LINCOLNWOOD PUBLIC LIBRARY

W9-BVR-669

Lincolnwood Library
4000 W. Pratt Ave.
Lincolnwood, IL 60712

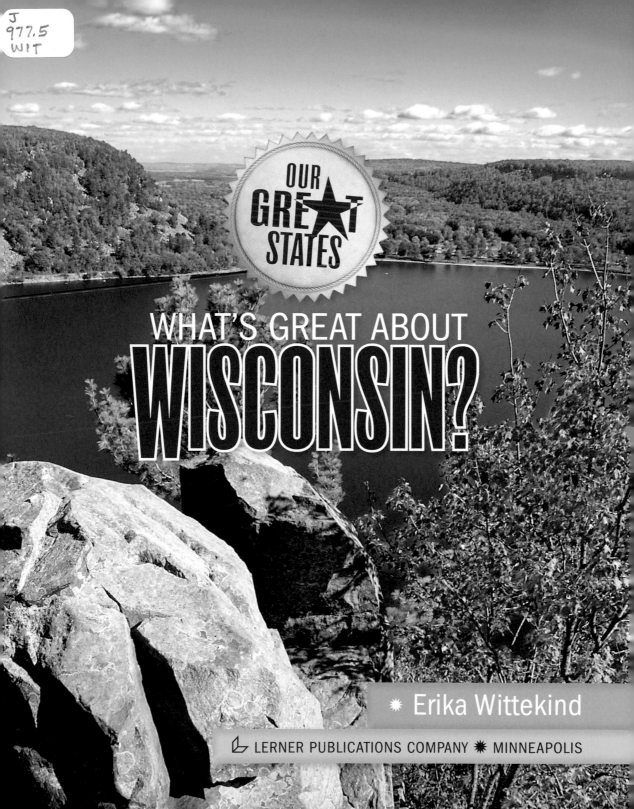

J
977.5
WIT

OUR
GRE★T
STATES

WHAT'S GREAT ABOUT
WISCONSIN?

✴ Erika Wittekind

↳ LERNER PUBLICATIONS COMPANY ✴ MINNEAPOLIS

CONTENTS

WISCONSIN WELCOMES YOU! * 4

WISCONSIN DELLS * 6

CHEESE * 8

ICE AGE TRAIL * 10

DANE COUNTY FARMERS' MARKET * 12

DOOR COUNTY * 14

Copyright © 2015
by Lerner Publishing Group, Inc.

Content Consultant: Patricia Stovey, Assistant Professor of History, University of Wisconsin La Crosse

All rights reserved. International copyright secured. No part of this book may be reproduced, stored in a retrieval system, or transmitted in any form or by any means—electronic, mechanical, photocopying, recording, or otherwise—without the prior written permission of Lerner Publishing Group, Inc., except for the inclusion of brief quotations in an acknowledged review.

Lerner Publications Company
A division of Lerner Publishing Group, Inc.
241 First Avenue North
Minneapolis, MN 55401 USA

For reading levels and more information, look up this title at www.lernerbooks.com.

Main body text set in ITC Franklin Gothic Std Book Condensed 12/15. Typeface provided by Adobe Systems.

Library of Congress Cataloging-in-Publication Data

Wittekind, Erika, 1980-
   What's great about Wisconsin? / by Erika Wittekind.
      pages cm. — (Our great states)
   Includes index.
   ISBN 978-1-4677-3390-8 (lib. bdg. : alk. paper)
   ISBN 978-1-4677-4721-9 (eBook)
   1. Wisconsin—Juvenile literature.
I. Title.
F581.3.W59 2015
977.5—dc23   2013049922

Manufactured in the United States of America
1 – PC – 7/15/14

MILWAUKEE ✳ 16

GREEN BAY PACKERS ✳ 18

CIRCUS WORLD MUSEUM ✳ 20

HOUSE ON THE ROCK ✳ 22

CAVE OF THE MOUNDS ✳ 24

WISCONSIN BY MAP ✳ 26

WISCONSIN FACTS ✳ 28

GLOSSARY ✳ 30

FURTHER INFORMATION ✳ 31

INDEX ✳ 32

WISCONSIN Welcomes You!

Many people think of cheese when they think about Wisconsin. People from Wisconsin proudly call themselves "cheeseheads." But Wisconsin has more to offer than dairy goods. This midwestern state has many restaurants. There are lots of museums too. The state also has lakes, parks, and dirt bike paths. Some of Wisconsin's most visited spots are in places where few people live. There are rolling farmlands and pine forests. Tourists flock to Wisconsin Dells to see cool-looking rock formations. They also stay at the water parks. Others travel to Door County to hear stories of shipwrecks in Lake Michigan. There is so much to do in Wisconsin. Maybe someday you will see for yourself! Read on to discover ten things that make Wisconsin great.

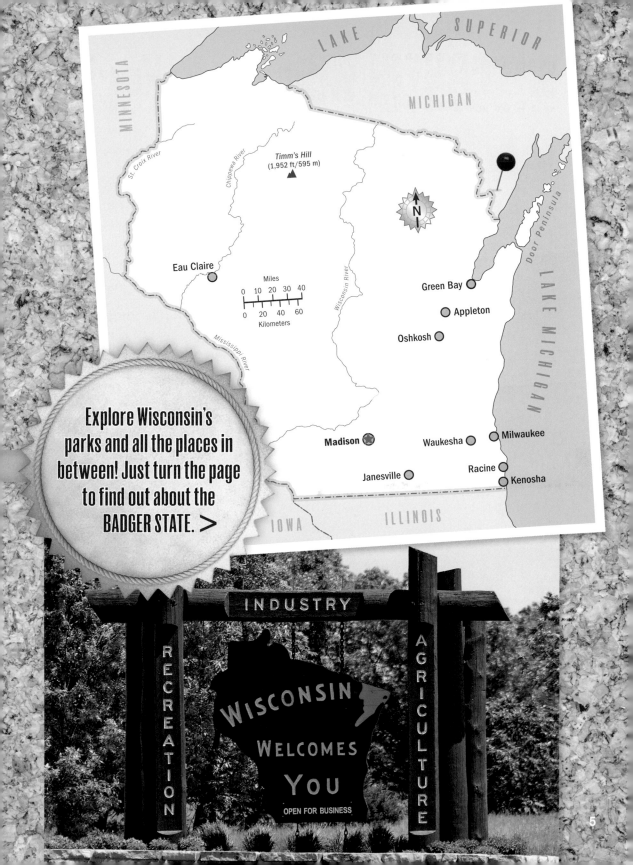

LAKE SUPERIOR

MINNESOTA

MICHIGAN

St. Croix River

Chippewa River

Timm's Hill
(1,952 ft/595 m)

N

Door Peninsula

Eau Claire

Miles
0 10 20 30 40

0   20   40   60
Kilometers

Wisconsin River

Mississippi River

Green Bay

LAKE MICHIGAN

Appleton

Oshkosh

Explore Wisconsin's parks and all the places in between! Just turn the page to find out about the BADGER STATE. >

Madison

Waukesha

Milwaukee

Janesville

Racine

Kenosha

IOWA

ILLINOIS

INDUSTRY

RECREATION

WISCONSIN WELCOMES YOU

OPEN FOR BUSINESS

AGRICULTURE

WISCONSIN DELLS

> Many visitors to Wisconsin head straight to Wisconsin Dells. It is the most visited city in the state! The city is near the Wisconsin River. The area has cliffs, gorges, and rock formations. Water from melting glaciers shaped the rocks. Glaciers are huge sheets of ice.

Take a ride on a duck for the best view of the dells. A duck is a type of bus. It can travel on land and in water. Many companies use ducks for tours. Ducks make their way through steep paths and deep gorges. They also float in the Wisconsin River.

Wisconsin Dells has more than twenty indoor and outdoor water parks. That is more than any other city in the world! The area has many amusement parks. You can also visit state parks, water shows, and museums. Do not miss the tour of the upside-down White House! This fun house looks just like the US landmark.

Enjoy the scenery of the
Wisconsin River on a duck tour.

WISCONSIN BUSINESS

Tourism is Wisconsin's
third-largest business.
In 2012, approximately
97 million people visited
Wisconsin. They come to
see parks, lakes, and other
places. Manufacturing is
another large business
in Wisconsin. Agriculture
brings in money too.
These are Wisconsin's top
industries.

CHEESE

> When is the last time you ate cheese? There is a good chance it came from Wisconsin. Wisconsin is the top cheese maker in the United States. More than 25 percent of the country's cheese is made here. This is why people from Wisconsin call themselves "cheeseheads." They are proud of the nickname.

Be sure to stop by a cheese store during your visit. You can try some of the more than six hundred kinds of locally made cheeses! Wisconsin has won more awards for its cheese than any other state. It is the only state to offer a Master Cheesemaker Program. You can take the demanding classes through the University of Wisconsin–Madison. No wonder Wisconsin is known for its cheese!

CHEESE FACTORIES

Wisconsin's first cheese factory opened in 1841. This is before Wisconsin was an official state. The state had more than twenty-eight hundred cheese factories by 1922. European immigrants started many factories. They made different styles of cheese. German Muenster and Italian mozzarella are two popular kinds.

Cheese is so important to Wisconsinites that some people wear foam cheeseheads during sporting events.

ICE AGE TRAIL

> Wisconsin is a great place to hike. The state has many lakes, rivers, hills, and valleys. Glaciers formed these land features. More than twelve thousand years ago, glaciers covered most of Wisconsin. As the glaciers moved and melted, they shaped the land.

Wisconsin is home to a National Scenic Trail. There are only eleven in the country. The Ice Age National Scenic Trail is approximately 1,200 miles (1,931 kilometers) long. It winds through forests, prairies, and state parks. It passes through lakes, farmland, and small towns. You might see an American Indian burial site along the trail. Look for giant boulders made by glaciers. The trail has signs to help you learn about important landmarks.

It takes experienced backpackers well up to three months to hike the whole trail. You can hike part of the trail in a day. Or spend a few hours exploring parts of a trail. You never know what you might see on your hike!

You will want to stop along your hike to read the informational signs along the Ice Age Trail.

Hikers along the trail will pass trail markers. This helps you make sure you're following the correct path.

DANE COUNTY FARMERS' MARKET

> Thousands of people gather in Madison for the Dane County Farmers' Market. On Saturday mornings in the summer, more than 160 sellers line the square around the capitol. You can buy fresh vegetables, plants, baked goods, meats, and cheeses. It is the largest producers-only farmers' market in the country. This means the sellers make or grow all the goods they sell. Do you want to know how to make a type of cheese? Or would you like to know the best kind of apple to make pie? The farmer is there to tell you.

Musicians and performers also love the market. You may see a ukulele player. Balloon artists make animals.

After shopping, go inside the capitol building. You can climb the stairs to the observation deck. From here, you have a scenic view of Madison and its two main lakes, Mendota and Monona.

THE OVEN $6.50
AD $5.00

The capitol dome has great views of the city.

FARM SIZE

Agriculture is a big business in Wisconsin. But the farms are often small. Most Wisconsin farms are approximately 210 acres (85 hectares). This is less than half the size of most farms in the United States. Sometimes big companies own many small farms. But approximately 90 percent of Wisconsin farms are family-owned.

DOOR COUNTY

> Door County is a popular vacation spot in Wisconsin. It is a peninsula that juts into Lake Michigan. Door County has 300 miles (483 km) of shoreline. There are fifty-three beaches. It feels like you are at the seaside in the heart of the Midwest!

The peninsula was not always known for its lakeside fun. At one time, many ships sunk in the area. Sailors called it Death's Door. Over time, the area became known as Door County. Stop by one of eleven historic lighthouses. Here, you can learn about shipwrecks.

There is plenty of fun to be had in Door County. Explore the hiking trails at five state parks. Or check out one of the county parks. Pick cherries at an orchard. Or eat ice cream at an old-fashioned parlor. You can even watch a movie at a drive-in. Take the ferry to Washington Island. It is approximately 5 miles (8 km) offshore.

Kayaking is another fun activity to enjoy while you're visiting Door County.

GREAT LAKES

Wisconsin borders two Great Lakes, Lake Superior and Lake Michigan. They are part of the largest freshwater system in the world. Wisconsin has more than fifteen thousand lakes. Together, they take up 20 acres (8 ha) of land.

MILWAUKEE

> No visit to Wisconsin is complete without stopping in Milwaukee. Milwaukee is a port city on Lake Michigan. It is a great place to fly a kite. Or you can rent a bike or a paddleboat. Milwaukee is home to many festivals. One is the Milwaukee Air and Water Show. It takes place each summer.

Milwaukee is a great place for indoor fun. It has many museums. At the Milwaukee Public Museum, you can walk through old Milwaukee. You will see the world's largest-known dinosaur skull. The Betty Brinn Children's Museum has hands-on art and science activities. You can make your own news show. The Milwaukee Art Museum has a display about fine art. There are hands-on activities for you and your family to enjoy every weekend.

Another fun place to stop is the Mitchell Park Horticultural Conservatory. It is also called the Domes. It's made up of three beehive-shaped buildings. They have plants, flowers, and trees from around the world.

No matter how cold it is outside, the Domes are always warm inside!

WHAT'S IN A NAME?

Milwaukee is Wisconsin's biggest city. According to many stories, American Indians named the city after the river of the same name. *Milwaukee* means "a rich, beautiful land." Many American Indian people gathered in the city.

GREEN BAY PACKERS

> Green Bay is the smallest city to have a National Football League (NFL) team. But the Packers have had much success. This has earned the city the nickname Titletown USA. The NFL created a playoff system in 1933. The Packers won three championships before then. They have won ten titles since 1967. This includes four Super Bowls.

The Packers are the only publicly owned major professional sports team in the United States. This means the fans own the team. Packer fans love their team. The games are so popular that people pass down their season tickets through family wills.

Tailgaters gather early at Lambeau Field. They grill hot dogs before the game. If it snows, volunteers help shovel the stadium seats. And when the game is on TV, football fans drop what they are doing to watch. Green Bay Packers games are a Wisconsin tradition.

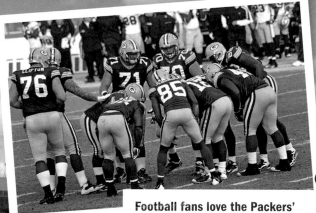
Football fans love the Packers'
classic yellow and green uniforms.

After a snowfall, Packer fans help
clear the bleachers before a game.

19

CIRCUS WORLD MUSEUM

> Circuses are not as common as they used to be. But the show goes on at Circus World Museum in Baraboo. See the daily show during the summer season. Each show has acrobats, clowns, and elephants. There is even a chance to take part. You can learn tricks and join the performers.

Displays show the history of circuses in Wisconsin. The famous Ringling Bros. Circus started in Baraboo in 1884. It was a traveling circus. It made Baraboo its winter home for thirty-four years. The buildings the circus used became known as Ringlingville. The buildings are a National Historic Landmark Site. The Barnum & Bailey Circus also was founded in Wisconsin.

The Circus World Museum holds the largest collection of circus items in the world. You can see more than 210 restored circus wagons. These wagons moved animals, performers, and props between towns. Fifteen of the wagons were used in the movie *Water for Elephants*.

This poster from 1899 advertises a show put on by the Ringling Bros. Circus.

FAMOUS WISCONSINITES

The Ringling brothers grew up in Wisconsin. Magician Harry Houdini also grew up here. Other famous Wisconsin natives include painter Georgia O'Keeffe and singer Justin Vernon of the band Bon Iver. Architect Frank Lloyd Wright and writers Laura Ingalls Wilder and Thornton Wilder are from Wisconsin.

HOUSE ON THE ROCK

> The House on the Rock is one of Wisconsin's strangest places. It is in Spring Green. Architect Alex Jordan built the house in the 1940s. It is on top of a sandstone tower. People wanted to see the odd house, so Jordan charged them admission.

Many buildings have been added to the original house. One building looks like a small town from the past. Strange items fill the buildings. One room has a sea creature longer than the Statue of Liberty. You can see dolls, clocks, and mechanical music machines. You also can see *Titanic* collectibles and carousel animals. Another room has model airplanes. You can see dollhouses in yet another room. There is so much stuff! You might have to come see for yourself.

Thousands of people come to see the House on the Rock each year.

This sculpture sits outside in the yard of the House on the Rock.

CAVE OF THE MOUNDS

> One of Wisconsin's best experiences is underground. Cave of the Mounds in Blue Mounds is known as the most beautiful cave in the upper Midwest. It is a National Natural Landmark. The main cave formed more than one million years ago. It was discovered in 1939. Workers removing limestone blasted the ground open. They found a large cavern. It opened to visitors a year later.

You can learn about cave exploring with a guided tour. The tour takes you to see cool rock formations. You also learn how the rocks formed. At its lowest point, the tour takes you 70 feet (21 meters) underground! Aboveground, you learn about mining by sifting for gemstones. Or you can join in a fossil-digging activity.

YOUR TOP TEN!

You have read about ten awesome things to see and do in Wisconsin. Now think about what your Wisconsin top ten list would include. What would you like to see if you took a trip to the state? What would you like to do there? These are all questions to think about as you make your own top tens. Make your top ten list on a sheet of paper. If you would like, you can even turn your list into a book. You can use drawings or pictures from the Internet or magazines to illustrate your book.

Take part in a fossil-digging activity after you're done exploring the caves.

> MAP KEY

- ⭐ Capital city
- ⭕ City
- ⬤ Point of interest
- ▲ Highest elevation
- –·– State border
- ━━ Ice Age Trail

WISCONSIN

1848

Visit www.lerneresource.com to learn
more about the state flag of Wisconsin.

LAKE SUPERIOR

MICHIGAN

St. Croix River

Chippewa River

Timm's Hill
(1,952 ft/595 m)

Wisconsin River

Mississippi River

MINNESOTA

IOWA

Eau Claire

N

Door Peninsula

LAKE MICHIGAN

Lambeau Field

Green Bay

Appleton

Oshkosh

Wisconsin Dells

The House on the Rock
(Spring Green)

Circus World Museum
(Baraboo)

Waukesha

Milwaukee

Cave of the Mounds
(Blue Mounds)

Madison

Racine

Dane County Farmers' Market

Janesville

Kenosha

Miles
0 10 20 30 40

0 20 40 60
Kilometers

ILLINOIS

WISCONSIN FACTS

NICKNAME: The Badger State

SONG: "On, Wisconsin!" by J. S. Hubbard and Charles D. Rosa

MOTTO: "Forward"

FLOWER: wood violet

> TREE: sugar maple

BIRD: robin

ANIMAL: badger

> FOODS: cheese, corn, milk

DATE AND RANK OF STATEHOOD: May 29, 1848; the 30th state

> CAPITAL: Madison

AREA: 65,496 square miles (169,634 sq. km)

AVERAGE JANUARY TEMPERATURE: 14°F (−10°C)

AVERAGE JULY TEMPERATURE: 70°F (21°C)

POPULATION AND RANK: 5,726,398; 20th (2012)

MAJOR CITIES AND POPULATIONS: Milwaukee (594,833), Madison (233,209), Green Bay (104,057), Kenosha (99,218), Racine (78,860)

NUMBER OF US CONGRESS MEMBERS: 8 representatives, 2 senators

NUMBER OF ELECTORAL VOTES: 10

NATURAL RESOURCES: sand, gravel, cement, limestone, lumber, water

AGRICULTURAL PRODUCTS: dairy products, livestock, corn, oats

> MANUFACTURED GOODS: metal goods, paper and lumber, automotives

STATE HOLIDAYS OR CELEBRATIONS: June Dairy Days, American Birkebeiner

GLOSSARY

agriculture: the job of producing crops and raising livestock

carousel: a platform that turns in a circle and has seats and figures of animals to sit on

dell: a small valley

ferry: a boat that carries people and vehicles across a body of water

festival: a celebration in honor of a special event

gorge: a narrow, steep-walled canyon

immigrant: a person who comes to a country to live there

manufacturing: making raw materials by hand or by machine

peninsula: a piece of land nearly surrounded by water or jutting out into the water

tailgater: a person who has a picnic in the back of a truck, especially at a sporting event

ukulele: a four-stringed small guitar made popular in Hawaii

will: a legal document that instructs how a person's property should be divided after death

LERNER

SOURCE

Expand learning beyond the printed book. Download free, complementary educational resources for this book from our website, www.lerneresource.com.

FURTHER INFORMATION

Allen, Terese, and Bobbie Malone. *The Flavor of Wisconsin for Kids: A Feast of History, with Stories and Recipes Celebrating the Land and People of Our State*. Madison: Wisconsin Historical Society Press, 2012. Check out this book to learn about local food traditions and how to make your own Wisconsin cuisine.

Environmental Education for Kids!
http://dnr.wi.gov/org/caer/ce/eek
Learn about Wisconsin's animals, outdoor life, and plants at *Environmental Education for Kids*! It is an electronic magazine for children that is run by the Wisconsin Department of Natural Resources.

Parker, Janice. *Wisconsin the Badger State*. New York: Weigl Publishers, 2012. This book covers all the important facts on Wisconsin, including biographies on famous people from the state.

Wadsworth, Ginger. *Laura Ingalls Wilder.* Minneapolis: Millbrook Press, 1999. Read this book to find out more about the famous Laura Ingalls Wilder and her upbringing in Wisconsin.

Wisconsin Folks
http://www.wisconsinfolks.org
At Wisconsin Folks, view the work of Wisconsin artists and learn about Wisconsin traditions in crafts, dance, food, and music.

Wisconsin Historical Society
http://www.wisconsinhistory.org/kids/#
Visit the Wisconsin Historical Society website's Just for Fun page for interactive activities for children. Find out how archeologists uncovered information about mammoths or solved the mystery of a sinking ship. Download paper dolls to learn what Wisconsinites wore in the past.

INDEX

Baraboo, 20

Barnum & Bailey Circus, 20

Cave of the Mounds, 24

cheese, 4, 8, 12

cheeseheads, 4, 8

Circus World Museum, 20

Dane County Farmers' Market, 12

Door County, 4, 14

farms, 4, 10, 13

Green Bay, 18

Green Bay Packers, 18

House on the Rock, 22

Ice Age Trail, 10

Jordan, Alex, 22

Lake Michigan, 4, 14–16

Lake Superior, 15

Lambeau Field, 18

Madison, 8, 12

maps, 5, 26–27

Master Cheesemaker Program, 8

Milwaukee, 16–17

Milwaukee Air and Water Show, 16

Milwaukee Art Museum, 16

Milwaukee Public Museum, 16

Mitchell Park Horticultural Conservatory, 16

National Football League (NFL), 18

Ringling Bros. Circus, 20

Spring Green, 22

Washington Island, 14

Wisconsin Dells, 4, 6

Wisconsin River, 6

PHOTO ACKNOWLEDGMENTS

The images in this book are used with the permission of: © Wirepec/iStockphoto, pp. 1, 10–11; © thoth11/iStockphoto, p. 4; © Laura Westlund/Independent Picture Service, pp. 5 (top), 27; © wellesenterprises/iStockphoto, p. 5 (bottom); © Andy Manis/Kalahari Resorts/AP Images, pp. 6–7; © Lorraine Swanson/Shutterstock Images, p. 7 (top); © Layne Kennedy/Corbis, p. 7 (bottom); © MaxyM/Shutterstock Images, pp. 8–9; Wisconsin Historical Society, p. 8; © Icon SMI, p. 9; © Jeffrey Phelps/Aurora Photos/Corbis, 11 (left); © ImageBroker/Glow Images, 11 (right); © Universal Images Group/SuperStock, pp. 12–13; © Snikeltrut/iStockphoto, p. 13 (top); © Henryk Sadura/Shutterstock Images, p. 13 (bottom); © DawnDemaske/iStockphoto, pp. 14–15; © photosbyjim/iStockphoto, p. 15 (top); © John Brueske/Shutterstock Images, p. 15 (bottom); © benkrut/iStockphoto, pp. 16–17, 17 (top), 17 (bottom); © Andy Mead/YCJ/Icon SMI, pp. 18–19; © Mark Herreid/Shutterstock Images, p. 19 (top); © Morry Gash/AP/Corbis, p. 19 (bottom); Library of Congress, pp. 20–21 (LC-DIG-highsm-12434), 21 (top) (LC-DIG-ppmsca-08401), 21 (bottom) (LC-USZ62-53798), 23 (LC-DIG-highsm-16717); © Independent Picture Service/Alamy, pp. 22–23; © ZUMA Press, Inc./Alamy, p. 22; © filo/iStockphoto, pp. 24–25; © markrhiggins/iStockphoto, p. 25; © nicoolay/iStockphoto, p. 26; © epantha/iStockphoto, p. 29 (top); © pkripper503/iStockphoto, p. 29 (middle top); © reelwavemedia/iStockphoto, p. 29 (center bottom); © Falombini/iStockphoto, p. 29 (bottom).

Cover: © Jonathan Daniel/Getty Images (Lambeau Field); © Wisconsinart/Dreamstime.com (dairy cattle); Wisconsin Dells Visitor & Convention Bureau (water slide); © Laura Westlund/Independent Picture Service (map); © iStockphoto.com/fpm (seal); © iStockphoto.com/vicm (pushpins); © iStockphoto.com/benz190 (cork board).